Counting in the Tundra 1-2-3

Aaron R. Murray

Enslow Elementary

an imprint of

Enslow Publishers, Inc.
40 Industrial Road
Box 398
Berkeley Heights, NJ 07922
USA

http://www.enslow.com

Enslow Elementary, an imprint of Enslow Publishers, Inc.
Enslow Elementary® is a registered trademark of Enslow Publishers, Inc.

Library of Congress Cataloging-in-Publication Data

Murray, Aaron R.
  Counting in the tundra 1-2-3 / Aaron R. Murray.
      p. cm. — (All about counting in the biomes)
  Includes index.
  Summary: "Introduces pre-readers to simple concepts about the tundra using short sentences and
repetition"—Provided by publisher.
   ISBN 978-0-7660-4056-4
  1. Tundra ecology—Juvenile literature. 2. Tundra animals—Juvenile literature. 3. Counting—Juvenile
literature. I. Title. II. Title: Counting in the tundra one-two-three.
  QH541.5.T8M87 2012
  577.5'86—dc23
                                    2011039560

Future editions:
Paperback ISBN 978-1-4644-0064-3
ePUB ISBN 978-1-4645-0971-1
PDF ISBN 978-1-4646-0971-8

Printed in the United States of America
032012 Lake Book Manufacturing, Inc., Melrose Park, IL
10 9 8 7 6 5 4 3 2 1

To Our Readers: We have done our best to make sure all Internet Addresses in this book were active and
appropriate when we went to press. However, the author and the publisher have no control over and assume no
liability for the material available on those Internet sites or on other Web sites they may link to. Any comments
or suggestions can be sent by e-mail to comments@enslow.com or to the address on the back cover.

♻ Enslow Publishers, Inc., is committed to printing our books on recycled paper. The paper in every book
contains 10% to 30% post-consumer waste (PCW). The cover board on the outside of each book contains
100% PCW. Our goal is to do our part to help young people and the environment too!

Photo Credits: © 2011 Photos.com, a division of Getty Images, pp. 4, 10; iStockphoto.com: © Bob Balestri,
p. 12, © Louise Cunningham, p. 20; Photos.com: frederic prochasson, p. 16, Hemera Technologies, p. 3
(oxen), Jupiterimages, p. 6; Shutterstock.com, pp. 1, 3 (petal, puffin), 8, 14, 18, 22.

Cover Photo: Shutterstock.com

Note to Parents and Teachers
Help pre-readers get a jump start on reading. These lively stories introduce simple concepts with repetition
of words and short simple sentences. Photos and illustrations fill the pages with color and effectively
enhance the text. Free Educator Guides are available for this series at www.enslow.com. Search for the
All About Counting in the Biomes series name.

Contents

Words to Know

oxen   **petal**   **puffin**

Arctic fox

Let's count!

One fox

Snowy owls

Two owls

Musk oxen

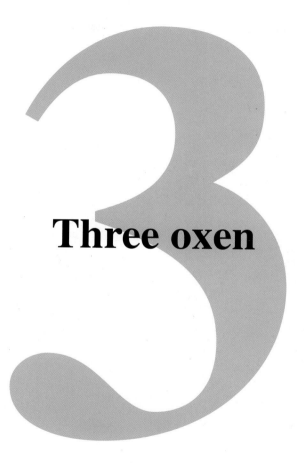

Three oxen

Polar bear

Four paws

Snow geese

Five birds

Pasque
flower

Six petals

7

Seven dogs

Atlantic
puffins

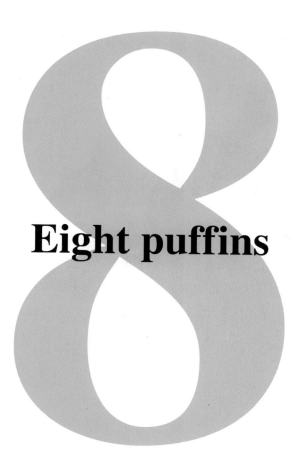

Eight puffins

Gentoo
penguins

Nine penguins

Grizzly bear
claws

Ten claws

Read More

Cefrey, Holly. *Tundra.* New York: Powerkids Press, 2003.

Marsico, Katie. *A Home on the Tundra.* New York: Children's Press, 2006.

Salas, Laura Purdie. *Tundras: Frosty, Treeless Lands.* Mankato, Minn.: Picture Window, 2009.

Web Sites

Kids Do Ecology: Tundra
<http://kids.nceas.ucsb.edu/biomes/tundra.html>
National Geographic: Arctic Animals
<http://kids.nationalgeographic.com/kids/photos/arctic-animals/>

Index

Guided Reading Level: A
Guided Reading Leveling System is based on the guidelines recommended by Fountas and Pinnell.

Word Count: 22